Step into Reading™

Quick, Quack, Quick!

A Step 1 Book

by Marsha Arnold
illustrated by Lisa McCue

Random House 🏠 New York

Into the barnyard
came a duck
and her ducklings.

All but one.

He stopped

to visit the baby pigs.

"Quick, Quack, quick!"
his mama called.

Quack started to follow.

Then he saw a butterfly.

"Quick, Quack, quick!"
his mama called.
"Quick, or the chickens
will eat all the corn."

Quack pecked
at a kernel of corn.
Then he heard the birds.

"Quick, Quack, quick!"
his mama called.
"To the pond.
It's time to swim."

Quack ate berries
along the path
to the pond.

"Quick, Quack, quick!"
his mama called.
"Into the water."

But instead
Quack played games
around a hollow log.
He danced on the log.
He hid in the log.

"Peep, peep,"
   Quack said into the log.
"QUACK! QUACK!"
   came out the other end.

Finally Quack jumped
into the water.

"Tails up,"
said his mama.

As the ducklings swam,
the sky changed
from blue to pink.

It was time to go home.
"Quick, Quack, quick!"
his mama called.

"Back to the barnyard.
Soon it will be dark
and Cat will go hunting."

Quack started to follow.
Then he saw
more berries.

One berry.

Two.

Three berries.

Four.

"Quick, Quack, quick!"
his mama called
from far away.
Quack had to stand
on top of the hollow log
to see his family.

But what was that behind them?

"Mama, Mama, look out!"
Quack called.
But she was
too far away to hear.

Quack jumped
off the log.
"Peep! Peep!" he said
into the log.

Quack's mama
heard a loud
QUACK! QUACK!
She turned around
and saw Cat!

Mama Duck
snapped her beak
and charged at Cat.

Cat ran away,
far, far away.
Quack's family
was saved!

"Dearest Quack,"
his mama said,
"for once I am glad
you were <u>not</u> quick!"